SELF-LOVE

Love is strong as death...Its flashes are flashes of fire, a most vehement flame. Many waters cannot quench it, neither can floods drown it.
(Song of Solomon 8:7)

SELF-WHISPER MEDITATION THERAPY & DEVOTIONAL POETRY

Release Negative Whispers From Toxic Relationships Through This 30 Day Daily Meditation & Devotional To Self-Love and Self-Transformation Whispers!

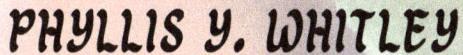

PHYLLIS Y. WHITLEY

Printed in the United States Published by Phyllis Y. Whitley on 6/29/2021
Self Whisper, LLC; WhisperVise Inc.
PhyllisWhitley.com & WhisperVise.org

This Meditation & Devotional Book Belongs To:

Name _____

Date _____

THIS MEDITATION THERAPY & DEVOTIONAL POETRY BOOK IS FOR WOMEN WHO STILL ARE CARRYING THEIR BROKEN WHISPERS OF PAST TOXIC RELATIONSHIP HURTS WITHIN. WHETHER YOUR PAIN IS FROM A RELATIONSHIP, CHURCH, FAMILY, OR JUST SELF-INFLICTED, THIS BOOK WILL INSPIRE & EMPOWER YOU TO LOVE YOURSELF AGAIN.

THROUGH DAILY AFFIRMATIONS AND MEDITATION, YOU WILL LEARN TO FEED YOUR SPIRIT BEING GOOD SOUL FOOD TO REACH YOUR SUBCONSCIOUS MIND WITHIN FOR A POWERFUL MANIFESTATION OUTSIDE OF SELF. PLEASE REPEAT, MEMORIZE & MEDITATE DAILY.

DAY 1

MEDITATION SCRIPTURE

And whatsoever you ask in my name, that will I do that the Father may be glorified in the Son

John 14:13

"The beginning of loving God is loving yourself the creation can't hate the creators."

— *Phyllis Y. Whitley*

MEDITATION THERAPY

Today, I let go of religious shackles that kept me in bondage and violated my flesh.

Today, I put on the clothing of Spiritual Sovereignty as I accept a life of freedom.

Today, I believe in the true power of God, and I look within myself to find Him.

Today, I stop the spells of religion and replace it with the Gospel.

Today, I take my power back from false leaders as I connect with my God within.

Today, I soak up the word of God all day long.

Today, I live my life in abundance, humbly.

Today, I am attracting the right people, places, and things to carry out my life's purpose.

Thank you, God, within!

DAY 2

MEDITATION SCRIPTURE

Death and life are in the power of the tongue: and they that love it
shall eat the fruit thereof
Proverbs 18:21

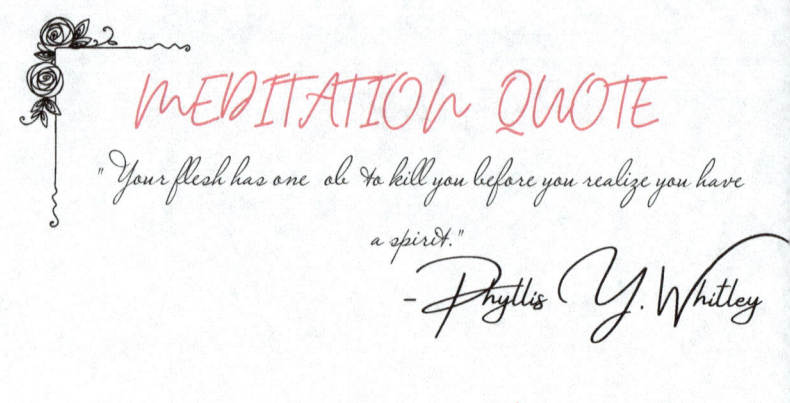

MEDITATION QUOTE

"Your flesh has one _ob_ to kill you before you realize you have a spirit."

— Phyllis Y. Whitley

MEDITATION THERAPY

Forgive me as I whisper to myself, the I Am, for not mastering my whole self in these areas: my temple, my faith, my wants and desires, my idols, and my worship. Forgive me for believing the lies that You and I are separated; thus, thinking unrighteous and falling short of your Glory.

I now believe and receive that we are one in spirit, and I am saved from lack of _____ through your son Jesus Christ who came to show me how to live abundantly so that my cup can run over unto others. At this moment, I choose life as I promise to use my kingdom keys and Godly talents to increase, multiply, and bring forth good fruits in my season.

I come back to awareness like the prodigal son surrendering my body, mind, and spirit to your higher laws. I consciously will think of good things as you order my footsteps to my promised land as I strive to have inner and outer conversations that are pleasing to your ears in hopes of yielding a good report as you flood my mind with your Holy Spirit to teach and comfort me. I will process the fruit of the spirit daily while embracing an example of kingdom life and leaving an influential legacy for my future generations.

Thank you for being my Lord, my Father, my King, my Truth, and my Higher Self. Amen!

DAY 3

MEDITATION SCRIPTURE

Call unto me, and I will answer thee, and show thee great and mighty things, which thou knowest not.

Jeremiah 33:3

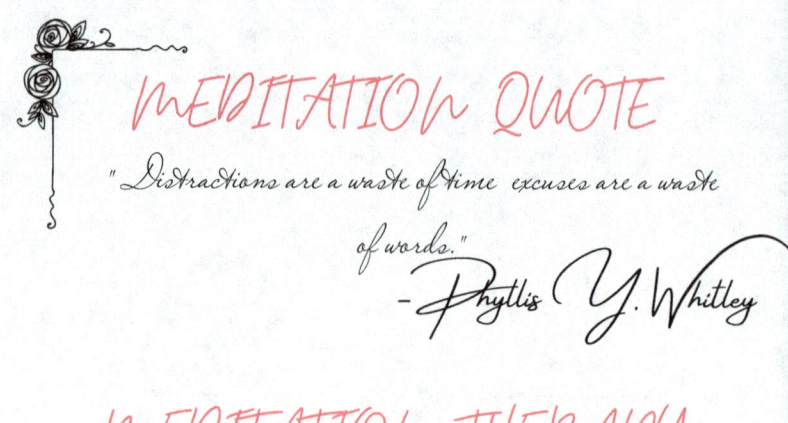

MEDITATION QUOTE

"Distractions are a waste of time, excuses are a waste of words."

— Phyllis Y. Whitley

MEDITATION THERAPY

Think a new thought (repent), live in Me now (belief), see no lack, and there will be no illusion. Be My book fulfilling your own chapters.

Be noiseless. Listen to your voice, which is My whisper. Learn of Me. Feel My being until you lose all that you thought was you, realizing it is really I.

Hush, seek and obey My voice. Release your selfdom as we do this together and watch Me give you the keys to My kingdom, which was lost within. All of the universe is waiting for your unlocking.

DAY 4

MEDITATION SCRIPTURE

Two are better than one...for if they fall, the one will lift up his fellow

Ecclesiastes 4:9-10

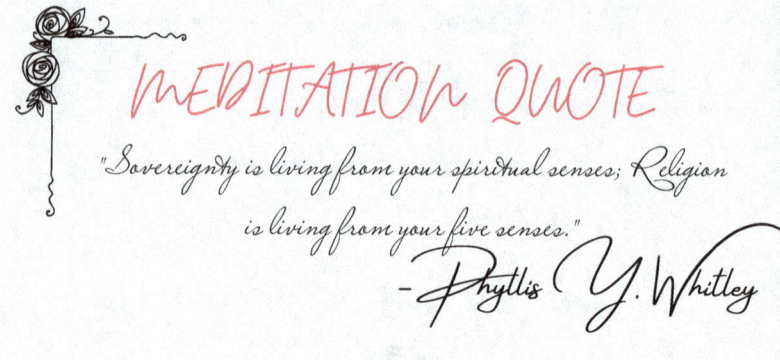

MEDITATION QUOTE

"Sovereignty is living from your spiritual senses; Religion is living from your five senses."

— Phyllis Y. Whitley

MEDITATION THERAPY

I Am your Teacher and Counselor, your Tutor and Advisor, your Redeemer and Rescuer, your Protector and Healer, your Guide and Driver, your Mother and Father, your Sister and Brother, your Friend and Business Partner, your Doctor and Lawyer, your Architect and Accountant. I Am waiting for you to accept and believe in Me to express and show Myself exceedingly through you from within.

Complete the sentences and become who you see yourself becoming:

I am _____(name a career)

I am _____(name your income)

I am _____(name your emotion)

I am _____(name your relationship)

I am _____(name your personality)

I am _____ (name your hobby)

DAY 5

MEDITATION SCRIPTURE

Love covers makes up for all offenses.

Proverbs 10:12

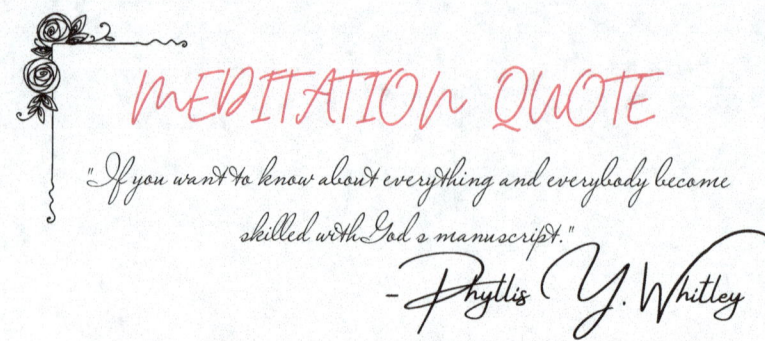

MEDITATION QUOTE

"If you want to know about everything and everybody become skilled with God's manuscript."

— Phyllis Y. Whitley

MEDITATION THERAPY

I release all religious shackles in my life's play.
I now let God produce my life's play.
I forgive those who willfully misguided my spiritual walk as I fire each character.
I forgive myself for believing in outside gods.
I replace my old religious shackles with divine spiritual sovereignty.
I am a unique spiritual being having an extraordinary human life role.
I rewrite my script by choosing my rightful role and the right characters.
Thank you, my innermost God!

DAY 6

MEDITATION SCRIPTURE

I am not alone, for the Father is with me.

John 16:32

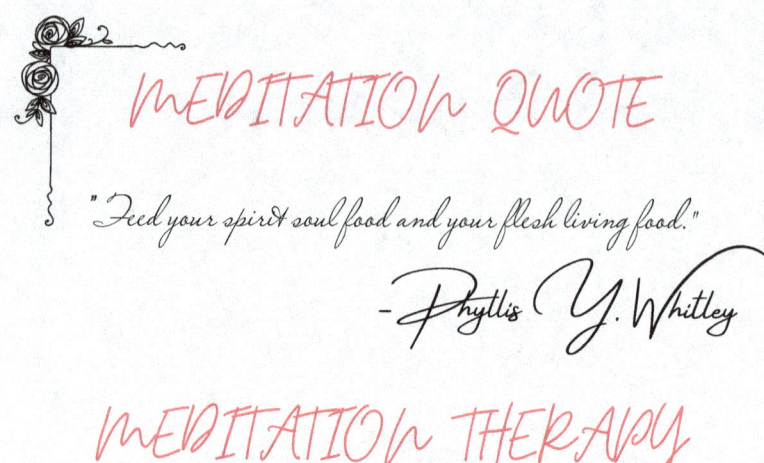

MEDITATION QUOTE

"Feed your spirit soul food and your flesh living food."

- Phyllis Y. Whitley

MEDITATION THERAPY

I now bring myself to higher consciousness.
I manifest unlimited benefits in my health.
I manifest unlimited benefits in my career.
I manifest unlimited benefits in my relationships.
I manifest unlimited benefits in my education.
I can see it, I can feel it, I can hear it developing within my spiritual darkroom of imagination now.
Gratitude and thanks to my unlimited God within.

DAY 7

MEDITATION SCRIPTURE

God is love, and he who abides in love abides in God, and God abides in him.

1 John 4:16

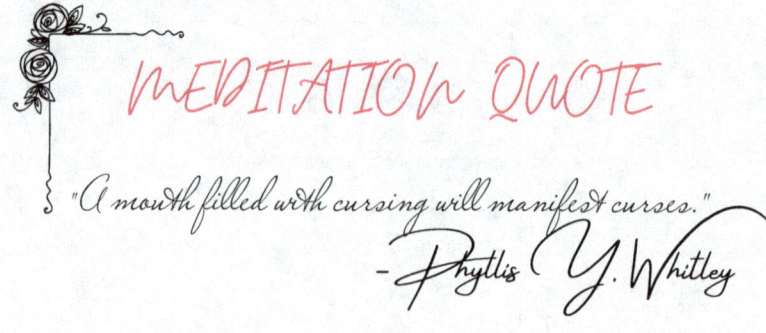

MEDITATION QUOTE

"A mouth filled with cursing will manifest curses."

— Phyllis Y. Whitley

MEDITATION THERAPY

I prophesy to myself:

I let go of my past pain as I now walk in my true divine bliss.
Every good dream of mine comes to fruition quickly.
I now go within my imagination and see myself winning in the game of life.
I am attracting the best specific people, places, and things into my experience.
I desire wisdom and humbleness to handle my riches righteously.
I rewrite my script every night to line up with happiness and peace.

My inner self is jumping for joy every time I give birth to my amazing desires.
I now unfold my unique God talents and gifts to become a blessing to all I meet.

Thank you, Divine Intelligent Father!

DAY 8

MEDITATION SCRIPTURE

He has said, I will never fail you nor forsake you.

Hebrews 13:5

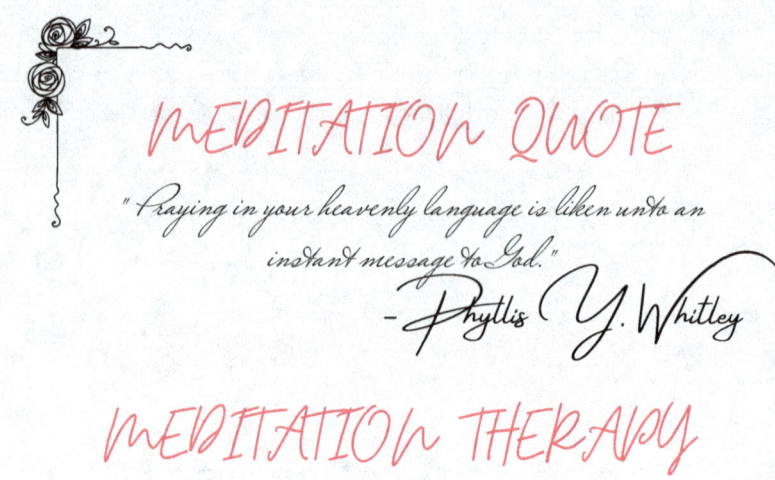

MEDITATION QUOTE

"Praying in your heavenly language is liken unto an instant message to God."

— Phytlis Y. Whitley

MEDITATION THERAPY

I am...

P rosperous in all things

R oyal priesthood

A dvancing towards my higher self

Y ahweh within

E xtraordinarily humbled

R evising my life play daily

DAY 9

MEDITATION SCRIPTURE

The people who know their God shall stand firm and take action.

Daniel 11:32

MEDITATION QUOTES

" *Respecting your garden, ladies, means not allowing every penis to sow into it.*"

"*Too many seeds in a woman's garden produces a weed of soul ties*"

- Phytlis Y. Whitley

MEDITATION THERAPY

I am now taking charge of my ultimate self.

I am enriching my garden every day by keeping a watch on my garden gate.

I am using my God-given power to choose the right characters for my fruitful life play.

I have decided to end soul-tie cycles and embrace my first love, God.

God is teaching me what a real king is because He is the King of kings.

While I am busy producing my play, I am attracting my soulmate, who is really me.

Thank you, Father!

DAY 10

MEDITATION SCRIPTURE

I call upon the Lord, who is worthy to be praised, and I am saved from my enemies.

Psalms 18:3

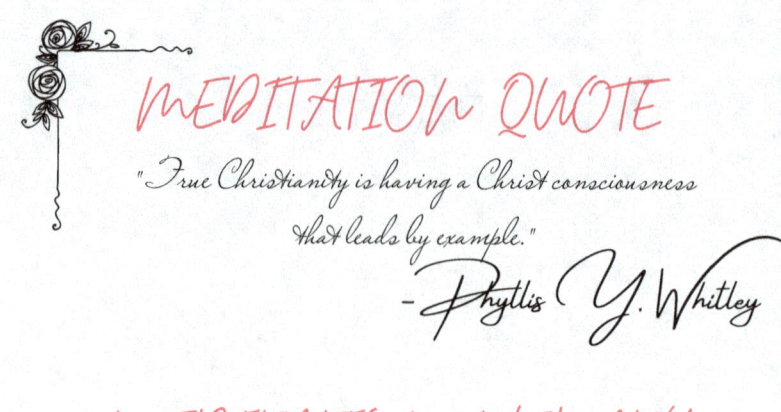

MEDITATION QUOTE

"True Christianity is having a Christ consciousness that leads by example."

– Phyllis Y. Whitley

MEDITATION THERAPY

I decree and declare that I am a happy, healthy, wise, fun-loving, patient, humble, and prosperous being.

I decree and declare that I am a loving light unto all I encounter virtually, physically, and spiritually.

I decree and declare I am attracting like-minded beings as we all love, live , and laugh in God's one-ness.

I decree and declare that my mind is full of abundance saving me from the illusion of lack.

I decree and declare that I am love, living under new management.

Thank you, Divine Glory within me!

DAY 11

MEDITATION SCRIPTURE

Beloved, do not avenge yourselves, but rather give place to wrath; for it is written, "Vengeance is Mine, I will repay," says the Lord.

Romans 12:19

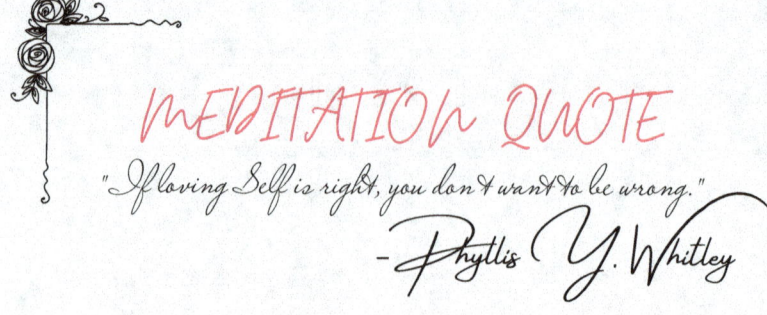

MEDITATION QUOTE

"If loving Self is right, you don't want to be wrong."

— Phyllis Y. Whitley

MEDITATION THERAPY

I release all the religious shackles in my life.
I now go to my Kingdom market within to buy all my spiritual makeup.
I now feed my mind with good soul food of thoughts.
I am now walking in my spiritual sovereignty abundance.
I am the person God ordained me to be.
I am using my mind to create my fabulous spouse and children.
My family will be my first platform to witness God's greatness.
I allow nothing but the best to enter the gates of my ears and eyes, and I wear only the best spiritual apparel.
I am my own candles of light.
I walk it, I talk it, I see it.
Who am I?
They all call me blessed!
But you can call me virtuous.

Amen!

DAY 12

MEDITATION SCRIPTURE

Charm is deceitful, and beauty is vain, but a woman who fears the Lord is to be praised.

Proverbs 31:30

MEDITATION QUOTE

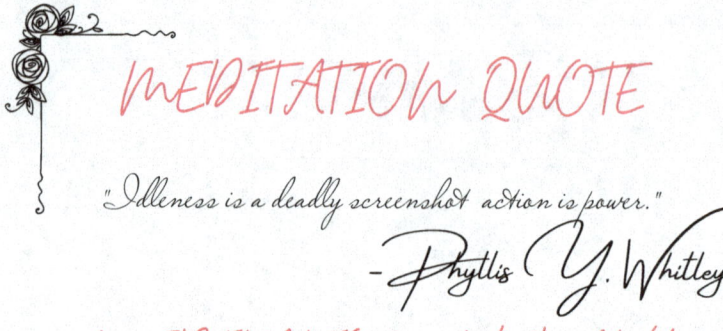

"Idleness is a deadly screenshot action is power."

- Phyllis Y. Whitley

MEDITATION THERAPY

I am enjoying every minute of our luxury European cruise vacation with friends and family. Yesterday we explored the land of castles and kings; it was breathtaking.

I can see how immense and regal the old castles stood and the beautiful rooms kings once lived in.

We are having a wonderful time sightseeing. Oh, look at those beautiful statues!

I am feeling warmth, love, and happiness all at the same time.

I can hear everyone laughing with joy as we all walk back to our luxury suites.

I cannot keep my eyes off the beautiful ocean view from our large balcony. I can smell the ocean water and hear the peaceful waves.

I hear someone knocking at our cabin door. It is room service delivering our family dinner.

It smells so good! I cannot wait to eat with my family. I am so full now and ready to end our night.

This has been one of my many fantastic vacations. I cannot also wait to tour Rome, Florence, and Venice tomorrow.

This whole trip filled me with so much joy and peace.

Thank you, innermost High God, for sharing your treasures with us!

DAY 13

MEDITATION SCRIPTURE

I commune with my heart in the night; I meditate and search my spirit.

Psalms 77:6

MEDITATION QUOTE

"Imagination is the house of your spiritual senses and your mind is the storage of your life blueprints."

— *Phytlis Y. Whitley*

MEDITATION THERAPY

I am liberated through truth and wisdom.

I am a magnet that attracts kingdom laws.

I am awakened to my true purpose.

I act as though I am that which my desire calls.

My words are cleansing my thoughts.

My thoughts are rinsing my mouth.

I am revealing the power within me.

My inward beauty is coming outward with a shout.

My respect toward others bounces back to me.

My tattoos are my unspoken words, so don't ask.

My scars are my testimonies with a sky.

I am my unlimited supply reaching above the sky.

I am the greatness hidden within me.

I am my spirit supervisor that oversees.

Prayer is my fuel source every day.

My God is the producer of my play.

Relax! Because Mastermind Jesus has the final say.

DAY 14

MEDITATION SCRIPTURE

Weeping may tarry for the night, but joy comes with the morning.

Psalms 30:5

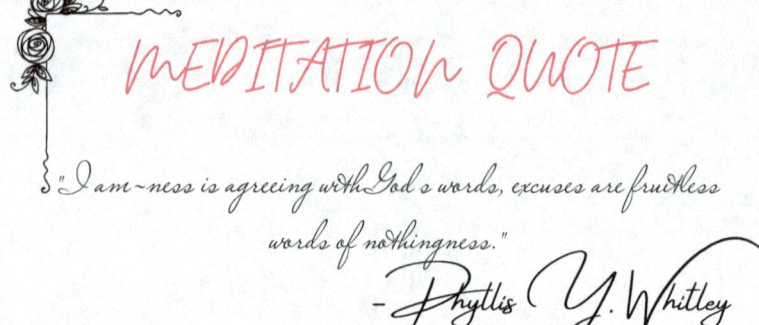

MEDITATION QUOTE

"I am~ness is agreeing with God's words, excuses are fruitless words of nothingness."

— Phyllis Y. Whitley

MEDITATION THERAPY

Thank you, El Shaddai, for being so almighty. You are my only El Elyon that cannot be copied because you are my master Adonai, yes Yahweh too. My actions are covered by my Jehovah Nissi, all wrapped up in one. Continue to shepherd me Jehovah Raah as you heal my old pain, Jehovah Rapha. I hear your righteousness Jehovah Tsidkenu and feel your sanctification Jehovah Mekoddishkem. My El Olam lives forever, and I am so glad you are my Elohim and my Qanna that let me know when you are jealous if I look outside of myself for you. No matter where I travel, I know that Jehovah Shammah is ahead of me because Jehovah Tsidkenu is purifying my steps. How astonished I am at my maker Elohim. Jehovah Jireh always provides for me while Jehovah Shalom showers me with peace and blessings for my whole household. Thanks be to Jehovah Sabaoth!

Amen.

DAY 15

MEDITATION SCRIPTURE

Blessed is the man who trusts in the Lord, whose trust is the Lord.

Jeremiah 17:7

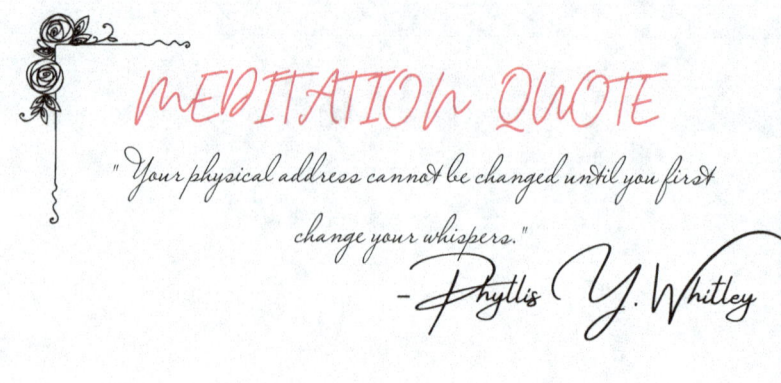

MEDITATION QUOTE

"*Your physical address cannot be changed until you first change your whispers.*"

— *Phyllis Y. Whitley*

MEDITATION THERAPY

I am that I am, visualizing my deep desire to come my way, but wait a minute, I heard that you where already here, so what do I do now? Wait or create? I think I will go within to find myself cleaning out the pollution and the clutter from my past tenants. Oh, how it hurts to feel the pain of letting go. I must replace my empty rooms, so I choose the furniture of joy, love, and peace. I now hear knocking at my door a host of my beautiful promises. I am excited to entertain my blissful company of delight; oh, it feels so good having faith and patience holding my hand while love smells up my fabulous being with prophetic whispers of truth.

Thank you, God, of the Highest!

DAY 16

MEDITATION SCRIPTURE

Anxiety in a man's heart weighs him down, but a good word makes him glad.

Proverbs 28:12

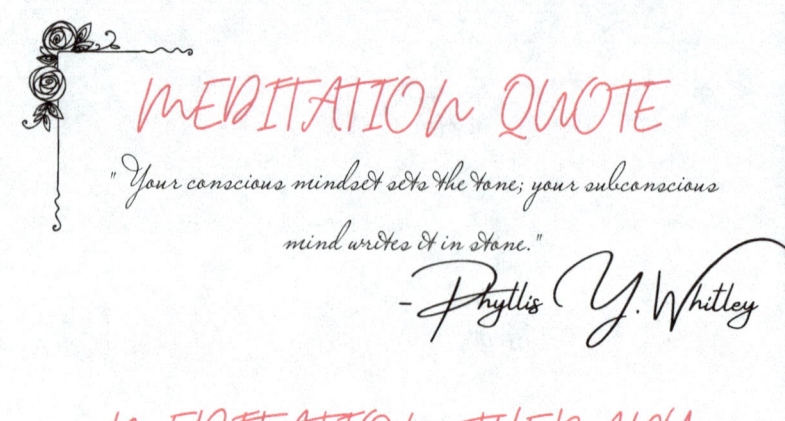

MEDITATION QUOTE

"Your conscious mindset sets the tone; your subconscious mind writes it in stone."

— Phytlis Y. Whitley

MEDITATION THERAPY

Every night and some days, I await Your love into my garden with rich seeds that I can soak up and cultivate. Then, I hand it to my Father God, who will make it visible so that our secret will be revealed. I trust that You, Father God, will bring the best seeds that will manifest into greatness where I can showcase them on my world stage play called my promised land.

DAY 17

MEDITATION SCRIPTURE

I keep the Lord always before me; because he is at my right hand, I shall not be moved.

Psalms 16:8

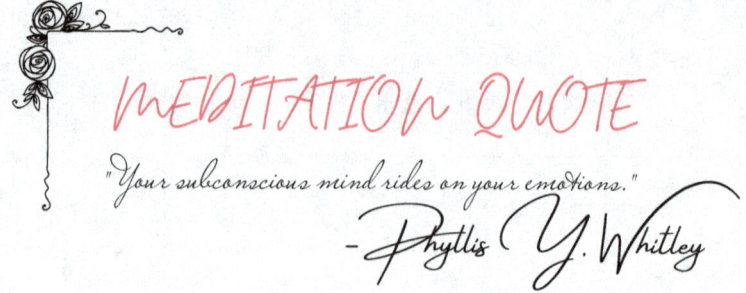

MEDITATION QUOTE

"Your subconscious mind rides on your emotions."

- Phyllis Y. Whitley

MEDITATION THERAPY

*As I look in my mirror, I see a **virtuous beauty** called me. My body is a magnificent, developing sculpture.*
I love my skin, shade, and texture; oh, how beautiful it shows on me.
Even my scars are my secret meanings revealing the uniqueness of me.
I smell so good, just like the flower that is really me.
I enjoy giving my skin what it needs as it talks to me.
Oh, how exquisite is my touch!
I choose who can share that special journey with me.
*My tattoos are my **silent whispers** beneath my skin.*
My smile is my candlelight in me.
My laughter is my medicine within.
My speech is full of sweet rhythms in me.
My eyes are mirroring my soul from within.
*My Father God is my true **divinity** in me.*
*Thank you, Father God, for revealing you **within** me!*

DAY 18

MEDITATION SCRIPTURE

He who restrains his words has knowledge, and he who has a cool spirit is a man of understanding.

Proverbs 17:27

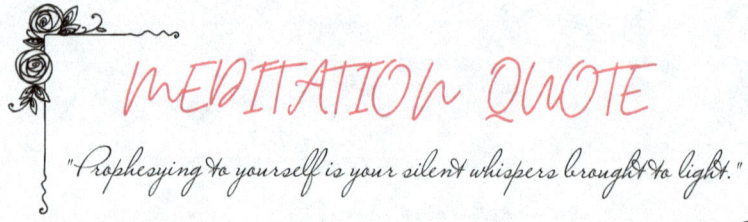

MEDITATION QUOTE

"Prophesying to yourself is your silent whispers brought to light."

- Phyllis Y. Whitley

MEDITATION THERAPY

As I lay down to sleep, my garden of Eden is secretly developing my inward vision of prosperity, fulfilling my like-minded mate into my life story now. It is done, Father!

Today and every day, my mind is downloading nothing but the best for my family and me, as we prosper coming in and going out. Thank you, my Brilliant Lord!

All my minds are on one accord manifesting my heart's desire of peace, joy, love, and laughter at this present moment. Thanks, Infinite God within!

I am receiving smooth flowing traffic of people, places, and things into my life right now on my beautiful stage of life; forever, giving.

Thank you, my Immeasurable God.

DAY 19

MEDITATION SCRIPTURE

He who gets wisdom loves himself.
Proverbs 19:8

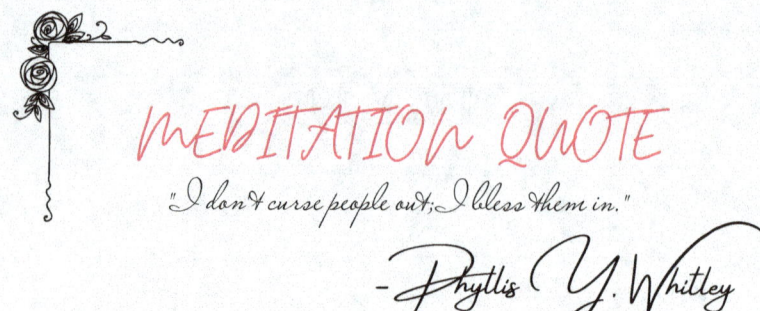

MEDITATION QUOTE

"I don't curse people out; I bless them in."

— *Phyllis Y. Whitley*

MEDITATION THERAPY

I abide in God's Word today.
I have decided to meditate on God's word
throughout my day.
I forgive and let go of all my limitations today.
Therefore, no lack, curse, voodoo spell, or negative
words can enter my house today.
Both my spiritual and physical houses are blessed
today.
Thank you, God, for overseeing my castle today!

DAY 20

MEDITATION SCRIPTURE

To set the mind on the Spirit is life and peace.
Romans 8:6

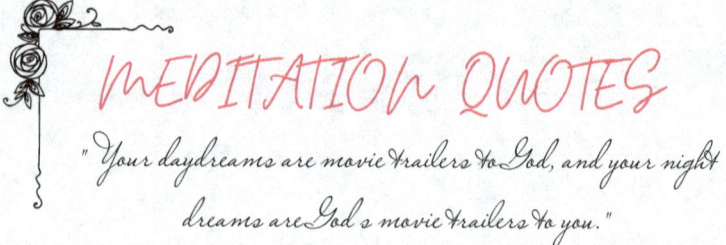

MEDITATION QUOTES

"Your daydreams are movie trailers to God, and your night dreams are God's movie trailers to you."

"Dream your blockbuster movie within until God releases it to the world."

— Phyllis Y. Whitley

MEDITATION THERAPY

My I AM-NESS

Who am I? I Am your pre-views

Who am I? I Am your dreams

Who am I? I Am your advertisement

Who am I? I Am your heart desires

Who am I? I Am your daytime snapshots

Who am I? I Am your night movie trailer

Who am I? I Am your blueprints

Who am I? I Am your life script play

Who am I? I Am your God

Who am I? I Am you

DAY 21

MEDITATION SCRIPTURE

Come to me, all who labour and are heavy laden, and I will give

you rest.

Matthew 11:28

MEDITATION QUOTES

"Yesterday can be your revision, and tomorrow can only be your reaction for today."

"If you stop producing fruit, then God will stop producing for you."

— Phyllis Y. Whitley

MEDITATION THERAPY

To everything, there is a season:

A time for every purpose under heaven: I am thankful for preparation.

A time to be born: I am being renewed daily.

A time to die: I am letting go of my past pain.

A time to plant: I am sowing good seed daily.

A time to pluck what is planted: I am removing all negative people, places, and things from my life.

A time to kill: I am releasing the old me daily.

A time to heal: My heart forgives my enemies.

A time to break down: I fell yesterday but I got back up today.

A time to build up: God lifts me up daily.

A time to weep: God is wiping my past tears.

A time to laugh: Laughter is my daily medicine.

A time to mourn: I miss you, but I must move on.

And a time to dance: I am rejoicing in my promise land.

Ecclesiastes 3:1-4

DAY 22

MEDITATION SCRIPTURE

Who shall separate us from the love of Christ? Shall tribulation,

or distress, or persecution, or famine, or nakedness, or peril, or sword?

Romans 8:35

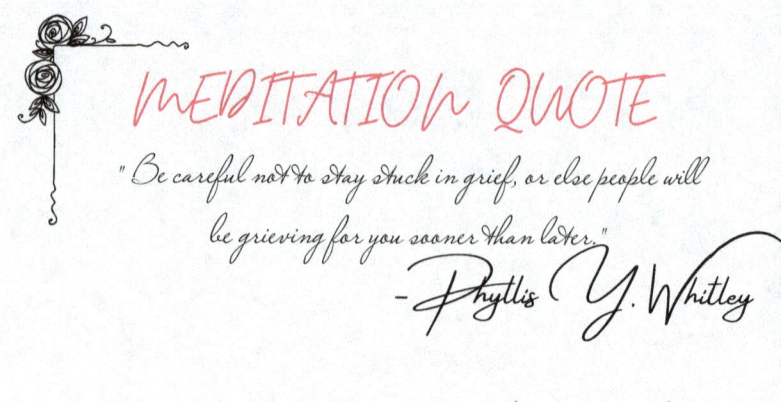

MEDITATION QUOTE

" Be careful not to stay stuck in grief, or else people will be grieving for you sooner than later."

— Phyllis Y. Whitley

MEDITATION THERAPY

This Morning:

I open up my conscious awareness to my heart's desire.

I open up my conscious thoughts to my desired visions.

I open up my conscious heart to receive more knowledge.

I open up my intelligent mind to perceive what's about to happen to me.

I open up my spiritual ears to hear only the   healthy for me.

I open up my spiritual eyes to see what God sees for me.

I open up my mouth to prophesy   truth to me and others.

I open up my fabulous future from today.

Oh, how I praise you, Lord, for all the new opportunities opening up for me today!

DAY 23

MEDITATION SCRIPTURE

The tongue of the wise brings healing.
Proverbs 17:22

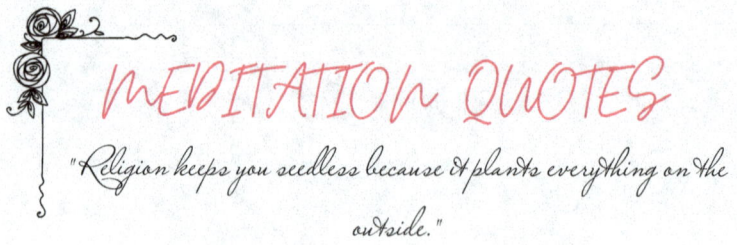

MEDITATION QUOTES

"Religion keeps you seedless because it plants everything on the outside."

"Seedless people produce only copycats and not originalities."

- Phyllis Y. Whitley

MEDITATION THERAPY

Tonight, before I enter unto sleep, I choose to sow good seeds I received today.

My conscious mind is planting my seeds tonight.

My subconscious mind is working 24/7 to manifest it while I sleep.

My God-conscious is making sure my seed will not return unto me empty.

Tomorrow, my seed will be revealed.

Thank you, angels, for bringing my abundant harvest while I lay down to go to sleep.

DAY 24

MEDITATION SCRIPTURE

The mouth of the righteous is a well of life,
But violence covers the mouth of the wicked.
Proverbs 10:11

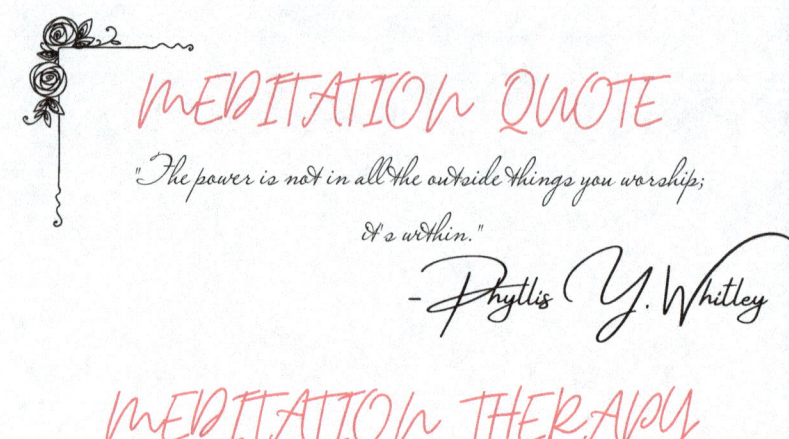

"The power is not in all the outside things you worship;
it's within."

— Phyllis Y. Whitley

MEDITATION THERAPY

Every time I let you go, you seem to come right back to me with uninvited guests. I recognize your friend's idolatry, drunkenness, and promiscuity waiting for an opportunity to be invited into my home. I will never forget how dissensions tried to come into my house and take over, but not anymore. I meant to ask you why your cousin gluttony follows me wherever I go; especially, when dining out.

This has been going on too long, and you must tell your twin couples of sexual immorality and moral impurity to stop trying to come through my gate at night. They are not welcomed here. Do not forget to tell the triplets depression, anger, and selfishness that I changed the locks on my door so they can stop waiting at my steps.

Now that I realize you were never a real friend because you loved talking about me to jealousy and envy behind my back; therefore, I release you out of my life.

I have a new landlord, named Jesus Christ! I am under a new contract with faith, and I welcome my new tenants named joy, love, and patience. Self-control, meekness, and temperance are also my new maintenance crew. I asked goodness, gentleness, and kindness to guide my house forever. Although most of us are hidden, do not be fooled, we see and hear everything.

I am laughing my way to freedom.

DAY 25

MEDITATION SCRIPTURE

Beloved, wish above all things that thou mayest prosper and be in health, even as thy soul prospereth.

3 John 2

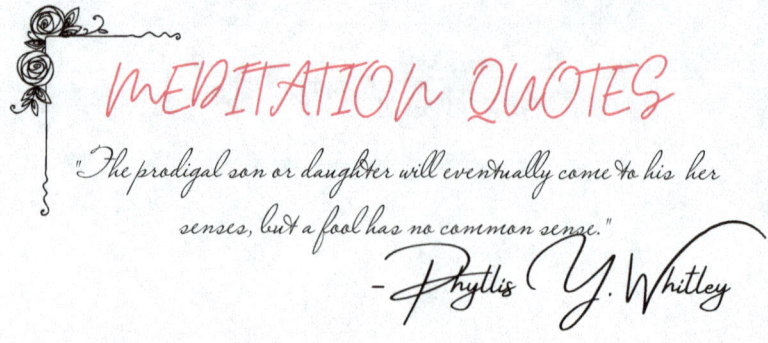

MEDITATION QUOTES

"The prodigal son or daughter will eventually come to his her senses, but a fool has no common sense."

— Phytlis Y. Whitley

MEDITATION THERAPY

It's so good to be home again, in the house of the Lord, where I belong. I am no longer traveling to see God because God is with me and within me. This is the day God has made, and I will let my smile be a witness to all that I encounter today.

DAY 26

MEDITATION SCRIPTURE

So then faith comes by hearing, and hearing by the word of God.
Romans 10:17

MEDITATION QUOTES

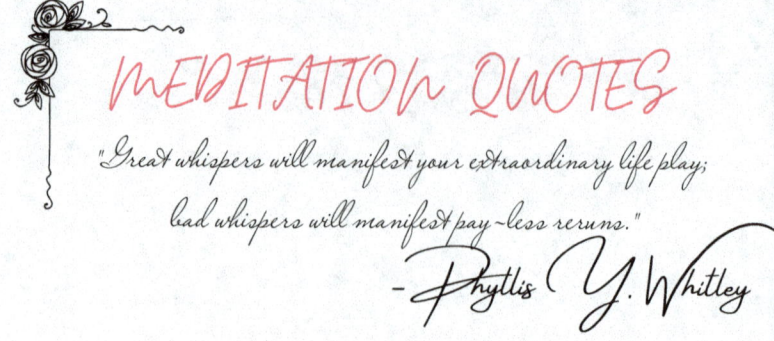

"Great whispers will manifest your extraordinary life play; bad whispers will manifest pay-less reruns."

— Phyllis Y. Whitley

MEDITATION THERAPY

Every day and every night
I revised my broken whispers of yesterday
Tomorrow will never be the same because I
learned how to train my words to match with
my thoughts in everyway.

DAY 27

MEDITATION SCRIPTURE

Whatever a man thinketh, so is he.
Proverbs 23:7

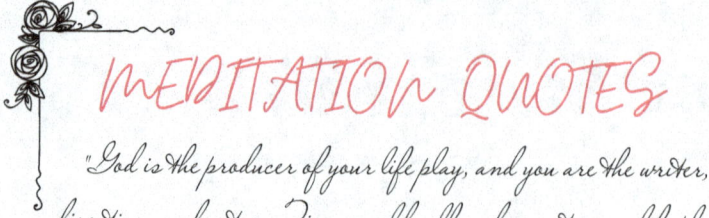

MEDITATION QUOTES

"God is the producer of your life play, and you are the writer, direction, and actor. Fire you old self and rewrite your life play."

-Phytlis Y. Whitley

MEDITATION THERAPY

I am writing my blockbuster movie starring me, myself, and I.
I have full power to cast out all the people who are not playing a good role for me to excel, so they must go!
I now receive all the right people, places, and things that generate the same positive rhythm as I.
My movie is sweet to my soul because everyone is now playing their successful role
for my legacy story that will be told.

DAY 28

MEDITATION SCRIPTURE

Ask, and it will be given to you; seek, and you will find; knock, and it will be opened to you.
Matthew 7:7

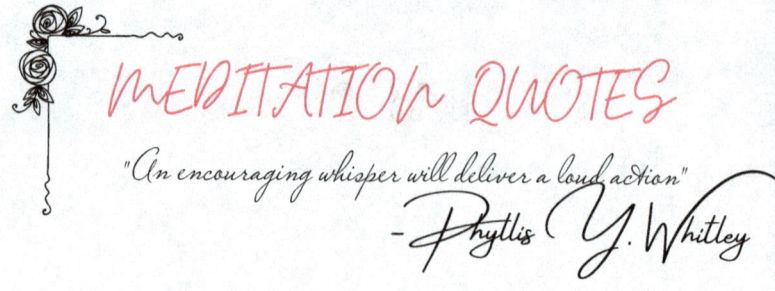

MEDITATION QUOTES

"An encouraging whisper will deliver a loud action"

— Phyllis Y. Whitley

MEDITATION THERAPY

Patience is raining on me with
Non-complaining
Enduring the illusion from others
being open-mindedness
persevering & persisting during difficulties
expressionless discontent
while finding no fault nor blame within

DAY 29

MEDITATION SCRIPTURE

I can do all things through Christ who strengthens me.
Philippians 4:13

MEDITATION QUOTES

"Self-love is the core of believing in the one who created you."

— Phyllis Y. Whitley

MEDITATION THERAPY

Planting My Wonderful Harvest:
My seeds are sown
My seeds are working
I will water my seeds with joy
I will water my seeds with peace
I give my seeds the sunshine of inspiration
I will keep my seeds temperature calm
I know patience will be my virtue
as I recognize & prune the weeds
I proceed to my next goals planting
despite having no visible growth
and just when it appears nothing is happening
my prayers have manifested my promised land that is now
visibly seen by all.

DAY 30

MEDITATION SCRIPTURE

When you pass through the waters, I will be with you; And through the rivers, they shall not overflow you. When you walk through the fire, you shall not be burned, Nor shall the flame scorch you.
Isaiah 43:2

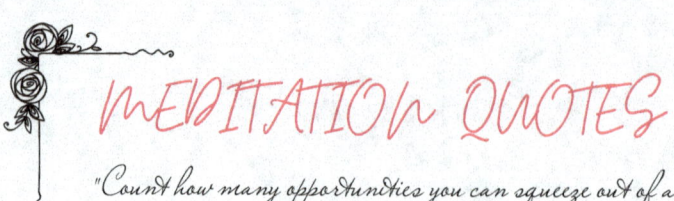

MEDITATION QUOTES

"Count how many opportunities you can squeeze out of any obstacles in your way!"

— Phyllis Y. Whitley

MEDITATION THERAPY

Today I see opportunities
Today I write my goals
Today I speak my plans
Today I choose to take a chance
so tonight while I am asleep
God will send out my angels
to bring all my desires to pass.

Finally, brethren, whatever things are true, whatever things are noble, whatever things are just, whatever things are pure, whatever things are lovely, whatever things are of good report, if there is any virtue and if there is anything praiseworthy — meditate on these things.

Philippians 4:8

About the Author

Phyllis Y. Whitley is a Holistic Relationship Consultant who has a continuous hunger to teach & empower women to revise their broken whispers into a voice of victory. Phyllis has produced many inspirational products on her website: phylliswhitley.com

Phyllis is also the author of Amazon #1 Bestseller *Spiritology.*